MW01110191

Foreword

I dare not speculate on why you may have picked up this book. Maybe you like the cover, or maybe you were prompted to read this book because the undeniable message of beauty tugs at your heart. You can't go wrong reading this book! "Beauty in the Eyes of the Beholder" delves deep into the core of where true beauty is found, and what beauty truly is. Many people are driven to look "beautiful" by the world's standards, but has any thought been given to what God says beauty is? He created it after all. This book goes beyond face value and brings to the forefront what God desires for His children to know about beauty. Your personal experiences may be very different than those talked about in this book, or they may be very similar, either way you will gain knowledge and understanding of what *true beauty* is. This book is not a novel or fairy tale, however it can have a happy ending-that part is up to you. The author, Jeanie Berry, is a very dear and personal friend; therefore, I know that this book is not something that she made up, she has lived it! And now God is using her life to speak to you. After reading this book, you will have gained an arsenal of truth to combat the tactic of the enemy that targets self worth, self esteem, and confidence. For me personally, this has been a great encouragement and enlightenment on God's idea of true beauty. This book serves as a solid reminder to look at the heart through love like God does, and see what He sees, in others as well as myself. The revelation in this book will change your life, *if* you will let it.

Josephine Blassingame
Crawford, Tx

You are a precious jewel.

I would like to **dedicate** this book to all the women who have at one time or another struggled with self worth, their appearance, acceptance, or feeling valuable.

I want you to know that man may look on your outer appearance and judge you accordingly; this is a part of life. There is one, however, who can see beyond your skin down deep into your heart! That is God. He loves you. He created you. He has a plan for you. My hope in writing this is that you find true VICTORY after reading this book. I pray that the eyes of your understanding become enlightened and you are able to truly see and understand more clearly who you were made to be in the image of God. I pray that the bondages that have entangled you will loosen and the grip let go of you and you truly become free to be YOU! For you are fearfully and wonderfully made. You are special and you are a jewel. You are unique. Though you may have fallen short in areas of your life, though you may have been bound by what others think about you, though you may have even found yourself having gone through a form of surgery to make your appearance better – your sins are forgiven! Enjoy yourself and who God has created you to be – embrace your flaws and focus on your strengths. Realize, God can work with you and make you so beautiful beyond your wildest imagination! Just open this book and have an open mind allowing God to reveal things to you. When something gets revealed or brought up, realize that is God speaking to you about your life and things He wants to help you with! Don't ignore it. Talk to Him about it. Let God take those things from you, heal you, bring victory to you, and carry on stronger! Be who God has created you to be and enjoy yourself! May you grow leaps and bounds and help others as you go through life. Amen.

Contents

Testimony – *Mended* from my Childhood!

I want to share a brief testimony of experiences about my childhood. I want you to understand things that happen to people while they are young can either make them stronger, or ruin their lives, if they don't allow God to mend the broken pieces. I want you to know why I was bound by beauty, bound by the way I looked, bound by what people thought I was supposed to be. I was hurt and taken advantage of as a young child. Because of all the sexual abuse that I kept secret year after year, as I got older I believed that boys had to touch me or show me some type of physical attention if they were interested in me. If I dated a guy that didn't show me physical interest, I thought something was wrong with me, or they didn't like me. Little did I know, they saw great things in me and were trying to respect me.

Many people who have had bad experiences in their lives remember some of the things that have happened to them and feel sorry for themselves. Some people find themselves turning away from God because they have blamed Him for everything that has happened. I want to shed some light on that darkness or mindset. It is not God that causes bad things to happen to us. We are His children; He only wants the best for us. The bad things that have happened in our lives are from bad choices we made or a bad choice someone else made that we had no control over. *Think about it:* Does your mom and dad put things in your life to hurt you? Of course not! So then why do we think our Heavenly Father would put things our lives to hurt us or teach us a lesson? He wants to give us the best gifts we could possibly imagine. You also have others who have been abused who are not able to separate themselves from their past experiences or situations. They grow up thinking that it's just who they are, not even seeing that there is a way to repair the damage. This mindset will lead them either to growing up hating people who have anything to do with what happened to them, or it will have the opposite affect and they will give of themselves *freely* because they are seeking comfort and acceptance. I happened to fall into this category of freely giving; although it could have been a lot worse than it was. I thank God for His hand on me throughout my life; through the prayers of my family.

I am sure, like my family, many of you have had those sweet baby stories that you hear over and over again at family gatherings. I too, have picked up on some interesting things about myself as a baby, toddler, and young child that I did not remember. I have done some funny and strange things as a toddler, I must say. I believe I gave my parents a "run for their money". I still have a hard time believing a couple of the stories I have heard.

My parents said I loved to play in my own "mud". Yes, you're guessing right! They said they would come into my room to check on me to see if I was asleep and I would have my diaper off, my "mud" smeared all over the bed, sheets, walls, and myself! EEEwww! I know, go ahead and get that out. It's okay, I'm over it, I can laugh at this now without getting a weird feeling in my stomach.

Well, another famous story about my growing up that they always loved to tell was the time I would kick the bars out of my crib and make my way towards my parent's room. They said they would hear my little feet pattering and they would say, "That had better not be

Jeanie Renay," and then they would hear little fast feet pattering back to my room. I would crawl into my bed and act as if I had never gotten out. I was a little squirt, I do believe.

I also remember being told when I was about 9 or so, I got my head stuck in the bars going up the stairs to the upper floor apartments. I guess I was playing and just stuck my head through the bars to yell at the people below, and guess what? I couldn't pull my head back out. My parents had to call the fire department and they had to grease my whole head and slide me out! Yes, I was a little rambunctious. And I could go on and on about all my softball memories. Dad and I had some awesome times. He imparted memories into my life that have brought me extra joy through hard times. Mom was always my cheering section. I thank them for being great loving parents. If nothing else, they got one thing right- there was always love in our house!

Looking back at my childhood, *those* are the memories I like to recall. Those are the memories that make me smile and I want to hear over and over. There are some other memories in my life that I am not so proud of. Some I could help, but some I could not. Those incidents caused me to have many questions growing up and much heartache, pain, and confusion.

I was told that I was a very pretty baby. Really I can't recall a time when people didn't say I was pretty. Please don't read that as haughty. I am merely making a statement to make a point. But what people don't realize is that **beauty**, if not properly understood, can sometimes lead to trouble.

I was sexually molested from the time I was about 5 until I was about 11 or 12 years old. There was more than one person who assaulted me, and it happened off and on all throughout this period of time. I remember feeling very nasty as I began to get old enough to know what was going on. I was always told not to say anything because nobody would believe me. I would be told that if I did, they would hurt me or hurt people whom I loved. Sometimes, they would say that it was our little secret that nobody would understand. *I believed these lies*, because molestation was all I knew growing up. It had become a part of my life at some point or another.

There were 5 men who sexually abused me and *only 1 of them was outside my family*. I knew that this was wrong, yet I allowed it to happen. I just thought it was part of how my life was. I began to *accept* that this is what men did to me. When I think about this place in my past, many different occasions begin to run through my mind. Thank God I have been redeemed, and the visions have been erased from my mind. But I know that sharing this part of my life is going to help someone out there become a voice in the darkness. Someone out there needs to know that although things are happening to them that nobody may know, GOD knows and it is <u>NOT</u> what He has designed for that person's life. Someone out there needs to know that they are *BEAUTIFUL* even though they may feel nasty and tainted with sins they may or may not of been able to help.

 There are about 2 incidents that damaged me for a long time. I remember being at a family members house, sitting on the couch, while the person was holding me. They were doing things to me under the covers, and his spouse was in the kitchen cooking and washing dishes. I remember just staring at them hoping they would see pain in my face, but I guess I hid it well enough. This happened a few times I went to their house. He was an alcoholic and every time the abuse happened, he was drunk. Finally, they split up due to his drinking all the time. So I got away from him and felt much relief.

Well, time went on and nothing else happened and I thought that part of my life was finally over. For a long time, I carried around guilt because of it, but now being over 15 years I have deeply, truly, and lovingly forgiven this person for doing what he did to me. I found out a while back that he has passed away, and the only cry I had in my heart was that I hoped he got right with the Lord. I pray that he found our Father's forgiveness for his stupidity and ignorance that we have also had at one time or another.

The last time I was sexually abused I was about 11, maybe even 12. I had a best friend that lived across the street from me. We would do everything together, we were inseparable. She was my best friend. But there was one thing my parents did not know, her step-dad had been molesting her and pulled the same stuff on me when I stayed. It went on for a long time and things that I never thought could happen to someone, happened to me! Her step-dad would always tell me not to tell anyone because they would never believe me, after all, I was just a kid. I wanted to tell my dad but I didn't want him to hurt him and then never get to see my dad again. I was so ashamed and I felt like I had let my parents down.

During this off and on battle a friend of mine at school invited me to go to church with her. I went, and I felt God's presence for the first time! I can remember sitting there and I felt like God was speaking to me and telling me that I can stop this from happening anymore in my life. I felt Him loving on me and telling me that this was not His plan for my life. ***I knew then, that what I was allowing to happen was not at all what God had intended for my life.*** Even though most of this was out of my control, there had to be a way out. God did not make me beautiful in man's eyes to be taken advantage of and messed with from every man I found myself alone with. *I finally put a stop to the abuse at age 12.* I had already told myself I had had enough and I stood up to my friend's dad one night and told him he would never again abuse me or my friend. Through God's strength and love, I ended up telling my parents and this man went to prison for the things he done to us. My best friend moved off with her mom and that was the last I ever saw of her. And that was the last time I was sexually abused.

I tell you this because I want you to know that *beauty* is so distorted in this day and time. Everyone is looking to be beautiful, to be pretty, to make a guy turn his head to look at them. But, if *they really knew* some of these lost men's intentions, if *they really knew* some of the thoughts that went on in some of their minds, I think they would be trying to do the total opposite!! I am not sure what happened to this man, if he is still in prison, has been released from prison, or even alive anymore. But I do know that I have released him from my heart. I have released and forgiven him for good.

It actually happened at our annual El Campo Faith Center Conference in 2009. I had forgiven this man with my *words* many times throughout my life, but I knew there was always something deeper that was hindering my marriage, hindering me getting closer to my husband, and receiving the full love of God through him.

Growing up, I had such a hate toward men. I always thought they were pigs, and did things behind women's backs. I really never trusted a man in my life, except for my dad. When I got married, I carried that into my marriage. I always had trust issues with my husband. I constantly questioned everything he did and his motive behind it. I made him and myself miserable! **But one night** at the conference, I went up for an altar call, thinking I was just going to get a fresh anointing of God. I can say that God had my number that night. Pastor Walter Ford, Pastor of Victorious Life Church in Victoria Texas, laid hands on me and said "That thing that happened to you when you were 11, it's done! It's over!" I still hear him leaning over me loudly repeating "*It's over, It's over! It can't hurt you anymore*". It amazes me when God uses people that know NOTHING about you, or things that have happened to you, to show you how much He cares for you. I felt a complete release from that night on! I remember just crying tears of joy for hours and trying to find a way to repay him for his obedience to the Lord. I honor and respect Pastor Ford and his precious wife Bonita. They are mighty ministers of God. I can't honor the Ford's, and not honor my grandfather in the faith, Pastor Eddie Cude and his lovely wife Bobbie, who are my Pastor's pastors. Everyone needs a pastor, even pastors. But one man and woman I could not thank enough, besides Jesus Christ himself, my Pastor, Pastor (Apostle)

Jeremy LaBorde of Gloryland Church and his wife Tamara. They have been there for me and my family many times. Pastor has helped me, prayed for me, been there for me, cried with me, laughed with me, stretched me, grew me up in the Lord, fed me, and is still looking out over me & my family. Not to mention his family, and many other people's lives. My husband and I have a wonderful Pastor, amazing church family, and we are continually growing in the Lord daily!

I am very thankful for the blood of Jesus Christ that has washed me, cleansed me, and made me whole! Jesus made me whole, just as He made the woman with the issue of blood whole.

> In *Matthew 9:20-22*, she knew that Jesus was her answer.... Desperate, she told herself:
>
> "If I can just touch the HEM of his garment, I will be whole!"

What faith she had in Jesus! God doesn't look at what we do and disqualify us because of where we have been. Christ's blood was shed for all of us. People disqualify us, we even disqualify ourselves at times, but **God never disqualifies us!** His Son's blood is made available to us at any given time, all so God can have an intimate relationship with us. Maybe you didn't go through what I did. Maybe you went through physical abuse, abortion, mental abuse, or something else. I want you to know that God is a healer of your broken heart! See, even though I know most of what happened in my childhood wasn't at all my fault, God was still there waiting for me to call on Him to help me through that time of my life. Praise the Lord, O' my soul, Praise the Lord. Those things are of the old, now God **has** made me whole.

INTRODUCTION

Everyone has their opinion of what it means to be beautiful. Carnally, we are looking all around us at what would **seem** to be beautiful. We are looking for man's acceptance with the outer appearance that God gave us, and overlooking what is lying within – our heart. If we don't like something about ourselves, we change it through cosmetic surgery, intense workouts, bulimia, diets, to the point of even starving ourselves; all to think it will gain others acceptance or draw their eyes toward us. All for what reason? Our outer appearance will soon fade away, but the word of God will last forever. It is truly all about finding beauty within, and there is only one way, through the word of God. It is through the eyes of the one true beholder. The God of the Universe. The creator of you. What is it that draws Gods eyes to you? What does God see when **He** looks at you? You can seem to have it all together on the outside, yet be falling apart on the inside. Are you ready to look in the mirror and like what you see, regardless what anyone else says about you? Well, with God, you can!

The saying *"Beauty is in the eyes of the beholder"* is a phrase that kept ringing to me over and over again. I could not shake it. It kept ringing in my spirit and every time I acknowledged it, there would be a stirring and a hunger to dig deeper on this phrase. The Lord woke me early one morning and spoke "Beauty is in the eyes of the Beholder". I said "OK, God that's great. What do you want me to do with that? "I tried to turn over and go back to sleep because nothing came to me the *brief* minutes I gave the Lord to reveal what He was wanting to say. He woke me again and said "Beauty is in the eyes of the Beholder." I started getting frustrated because I already tried this once and I didn't get anywhere except about 20 minutes of less sleep. So I said to the Lord "OK I'm up!" So I got up, grabbed my notebook and a pen, and started off to the computer. I googled the phrase that so sweetly kept ringing in my spirit and got some interesting feedback that I will share later on. I felt at peace and searched until that stirring was gone. So I went back to bed and slept peacefully.

The next morning, I was wondering what that was all about. I began to pray but nothing really came to me, so I ended up putting the information on the shelf and knew that one day the Lord was going to ask for it. A few weeks went by and I felt another stirring in my spirit with the phrase once again popping up into my mind "Beauty is in the Eyes of the Beholder." Already going through this once, I *immediately* responded with my notebook, a pen and my computer! I began to search some more and dug a little deeper on this.

The Lord began to share with me some awesome revelation on this phrase we so blindly use. I started to get excited about what God was wanting to do!

So I really began to listen.

And with that, came a flood of revelation of what beauty was all about. I would like to share what the Lord revealed to me about true beauty. If you are willing to listen, He is willing to pour it out to you too!

"Don't be ashamed to be who God has made YOU to be!"
~ Jeanie Berry

Chapter 1

Beauty in its simplicity

Beauty. What exactly is the defining of this word?

Beauty in the natural eye:

Those qualities which are *most pleasing to the* eye; a particular grace or charm; a beautiful woman.

Beauty in the eyes of God:

A clean heart set apart from the world. A place where He sits on the throne, where His love is shed abroad. It has qualities which are *most pleasing to the Lord*. It is holy and acceptable in the eyes of the one whom has created you. Beauty to God is the one who honors Him with their life and words. One who has been in His presence, with humility and meekness.

The word *beauty* has many women today starving themselves and much of the time, depressed, and left unsatisfied. I can admit, being a woman, we can find it easy to get distracted and caught up with our appearance and how we look to the world today. If you're not keeping your vertical relationship close, meaning your relationship with the Lord, it could really take a toll on you. Keeping your relationship close and intimate with the Lord is where you will find your strength and victory in any area of your life. Being caught up in how you look is a steady thorn in a woman's side, not to mention, the fear that tries to grip you. The fear that you're not good enough, that you don't look pretty enough, you're not skinny enough, you don't dress good enough, your body isn't "hot" enough, or even that the person you are with doesn't accept you nor is satisfied with the way you look. With these lies, you begin to think and believe that they are out looking and searching for something better. And since there is no pleasing them, they must be out pleasing themselves.

Through the steady thoughts given over to the enemy, you begin to get tormented in your mind. The bible says in 2 Corinthians 10:5 to "*take every thought captive to the obedience of Christ ..*" Everywhere you turn there are images, billboards, magazines, TV shows, movies, hollywood stars, even that neighbor that is flaunting herself, all showing you the worlds eye of beauty and what is accepted and what is not. This has caused a major struggle for women, as well as men, all across the world.

Women struggle by focusing too much on their appearance, trying to look a certain way, fix their hair a certain way, dress a certain way, walk, talk, eat ALL a certain way! Men that get caught up in this find themselves struggling with pornography, lust, and deception. What lack of freedom, right? Women have many struggles with insecurities, rejection, jealousy, pride, depression, the list could go on, and the root of it all is they have sided with the enemies *lies* about what makes them beautiful. With the world promoting really skinny women, whom *many* have had some type of cosmetic surgery to appear "perfect", and businesses using these "perfect" images to bring attention to their business, or families, no wonder many women are in bondage today! There are many times in my past that I was caught up in the way I looked. It was so bad at one time that if I didn't like what I saw in the mirror, I would not leave my house to go anywhere. I was bound by other people's opinions on what beauty was. If I didn't think I was measuring up to the world's standards I was not happy, or satisfied, with myself. You see, I was in beauty pageants, did a little modeling, and just really wanted to be seen. I wanted to hear how pretty I was because I had heard it all my life. Growing up, I was complimented very often on my appearance, whether it be what I was wearing, how my hair looked, how my makeup looked, even how my body looked. Because of this, I came to a place where when I went somewhere I began *to expect* to hear compliments on my appearance. If for some reason I did not get one, I would immediately begin to look at myself and see my flaws or think I was losing my touch *or beauty*. I even remember times where I would put on an outfit and literally stand in the mirror and make faces I would normally make to see what I looked like. I would turn around almost falling over to see what my calves or legs looked like in an outfit, and even had times where I would bend over in front of a mirror to make sure I had a little showing if I was to bend over in front of someone, and just how my upper area looked to other people that would be seeing it. I'M TELLING YOU, BONDAGE! I would turn all kinds of ways to look at myself at every possible angle. I was so consumed with other people's thoughts about me that I let it dictate my whole being. Although I lived my life thinking I was pleasing myself and everyone around me by trying to be as perfect as I could be, I was a very miserable, sad, and lonely person. It only brought me the bondage of depression, rejection, competiveness, major insecurities, and just living a life in chains! If we will let God come in and sweep away all the filth in our lives, we can be beautiful in *His eyes.*

I am so thankful that through this cleansing process, I now am free of all of this bondage! Getting compliments from people just make me acknowledge God more than ever, because I know that without Him, I am nothing! I know that when they are complimenting me, it is really my heart they truly see and it is shining for my Savior who has rescued me.

Having a beautiful sweet daughter has caused me to be reminded daily of this beauty. I tell my daughter many times when someone compliments her, "I know they like how you've dressed and look on the outside. But, how is your heart? Remember, you can be beautiful on the outside but if you're treating people ugly and rude, you will not **truly** be beautiful." Always look at your heart and make sure that no matter what you have on & look like on the outside, that your **heart** is beautiful! Your heart is where your truly beauty lies. It lies on the inside of you. I find myself hearing her make statements when she is complimented and told she's pretty. My 5 year old daughter will say "Yep! And my heart is pretty too!"

Because of man's sin (Adam & Eve) we were born sinners, separated from God. In *Ezekiel 16:3-14*, God takes us through a process of where we were when we were born and what He did for us! Let's look at it.

It states:
"(3)Thus says the Lord God to Jerusalem: "Your birth and your nativity are from the land of Canaan; your father was an Amorite and your mother a Hittite. (4) As for your nativity, on the day you were born your navel chord was not cut, nor were you washed in water to cleanse you; you were not rubbed with salt nor wrapped in swaddling clothes. (5) No eye pitied you, to do any of these things for you, to have compassion on you ; but you were thrown out into the open field, when you yourself were loathed on the day you were born." (NKJV)

As you know, we were all born into sin. We all are born separated from God. Sin separates us from Him. You see, His love for us is so deep and so intense that He wanted an intimacy with us. He wanted to give us the opportunity for **Him** to change us and give us eternal life. This is why He sent His Son to redeem us to Him, where He could wash us, cleanse us, heal us, and sanctify us to be His children. And give us an authority and power over the enemy who is after our souls.

It goes on to state:(6) And when I PASSED BY you and saw you struggling in your own blood, I said to you in your blood "Live! Yes, I said to you in your blood, Live!" (7) I made you thrive like a plant in the field; and you grew, matured, and became very **beautiful**. You're breasts were formed, and your hair grew, and you were naked and bare. (8) When I passed by you again and looked upon you, indeed your time was the time of love; so I spread my wing over you and covered your nakedness. Yes, I swore an oath to you and entered into a covenant with you, and you became Mine," says the Lord God. (9)Then *I washed you in water; yes, I thoroughly washed off your blood, and I anointed you with oil. I clothed you in embroidered cloth and gave you sandals of badger skin; I clothed you with fine lined and covered you with silk. (11) I adorned you with ornaments, put bracelets on your wrists, and a chain on your neck. (12) I put a jewel in your nose, earrings in your ears, and a **beautiful crown** on your head. (13)*Thus you were adorned with gold and silver, and your clothing was of fine linen, silk, an embroidered cloth. You ate pastry of fine flour, honey, and oil. YOU WERE **EXCEEDINGLY BEAUTIFUL**, and succeeded to <u>ROYALTY</u>. (14) Your fame went out among the nations because of your *beauty*, for **it was <u>perfect</u> through My splendor which <u>I had bestowed on you</u>**," says the Lord God. (emphasis added).

I truly felt beautiful when I allowed the Lord to cleanse me of all the filth that went on in my life. I felt the Lord meet me where I was and begin to pick me up from my own blood and clean me up. From there, I felt Him clothing me with all He had for me and when He was done, I truly felt like a beautiful crown was placed on my head, and I became <u>ROYALTY</u>! This is a good example of what God wants to do in our lives. Yes, we may have made some mistakes and caused some great heartache and pain, but God is no respecter of person, and what He did for me, He wants to do for you! We can be the glory of who He is, and through that, we can experience a life of total fulfillment which we have been created to have.

"It doesn't matter what the world says about you, what does GOD say?"
~ Jeanie Berry

GOD has made you Royalty. You are a child of *the* King!
......always remember that.....

Chapter 2

Ugliness in your life

ug·ly

adj. **ug·li·er, ug·li·est**

   1. **Displeasing to the eye**; unsightly.

     2. a. Repulsive or **offensive**; objectionable: *an ugly remark.*
       b. *Chiefly Southern U.S.* **Rude**: *Don't be ugly with me.*

"The words you speak may be uglier than the shirt your're wearing!"

~ Jeanie Berry

There are people all over the world that continually look and judge others according to what they *see*. There are people that see "issues" in people's lives and don't want to be around them because of how filthy they *seem* to be. It doesn't matter who you are, you are being tried by the enemy, and there are some people who give themselves over to the lies of the enemy, and there are others that combat it with the word of God, our weapon in life.

Everyone has some type of ugliness in their life. But we can become clean and beautiful by the blood of Jesus Christ. Hallelujah. It takes giving yourself over to the Lord every day, examining your heart to see if there is anything unclean within you. If you come across something ugly, you should have the **desire** to see it <u>removed</u>.

 In Luke chapter 8, there is a woman with an issue that she had for 12 years. I know I carried around an issue for a long time. Doctors were not my answer. Counseling was not my answer. It was Jesus. He was the only one who could truly help me. Maybe you have an issue you've been living with for a while and feel like giving up. Don't! The woman had her issue for 12 years! Can you imagine facing an issue that long? We face issues longer than a week and already feel like giving up. But this woman didn't give up. She knew where her answer was, and how she could become whole, clean, and beautiful!

[43] And a woman who had suffered from a flow of blood for twelve years [a]*and had spent all her living upon physicians*, and could not be healed by anyone,

[44] Came up behind Him and touched the fringe of His garment, and immediately her flow of blood ceased.

^{45} And Jesus said, Who is it who touched Me? When all were denying it, Peter [b]*and those who were with him* said, Master, the multitudes surround You *and* press You on every side!

^{46} But Jesus said, Someone did touch Me; for I perceived that [healing] power has gone forth from Me.

^{47} And when the woman saw that she had not escaped notice, she came up trembling, and, falling down before Him, she declared in the presence of all the people for what reason she had touched Him and how she had been instantly cured.

^{48} And He said to her, Daughter, your faith (your confidence and trust in Me) has made you well! Go (enter) [c]into peace ([d]untroubled, undisturbed well-being).

Luke 8:43-48 Amplified

This story always gives me hope and brings me back to remembrance of what **my** faith can do! Imagine if you were bleeding constantly for 12 years. You went to doctors and paid all the money you had to see if there was anyone that could cure your disease, only to find there were none. In Matthew 9:20 it actually says "she said to herself, If only I may touch His garment, I shall be made well." It said in Luke, that when she touched the border of His garment, IMMEDIATELY her issue of blood stopped! Jesus said "Who touched me?" He was in the middle of a large crowd. There were so many people pressed up against each other and this woman didn't even touch His body, only the border of His garment. And He felt it! He said He felt *virtue or power come out of Him!* That is the power of our God! And He said to her, "your faith has made you whole." It was her faith that she knew and recognized Him as the one who could heal her. It was her faith that pressed through a crowd and brought her issue with her **despite** what other people thought. It was her faith that pushed her way through to where Jesus was. It was her faith that said If ONLY I can just touch the hem of His garment. You see, she knew **without a doubt** that all she had to do was reach out and touch His garment and she would receive what she needed. She didn't' say if I could just touch "Him". She knew every part of Him, including His clothes, was anointed and carried the power she needed. That is powerful, and something we all can learn from. We are all faced with different problems, situations, issues, or circumstances that try to keep us bound up. Ugliness that tries to keep us locked down to guilt and shame. Just like this woman, our way out is our faith in Jesus! It is **by faith** that with Him we will move mountains!

> "If you have faith as a grain of mustard seed,
> you shall say unto this mountain, Remove
> hence to yonder place; and it shall remove;
> and nothing shall be impossible unto you."
> Matthew 17:20

 We have to have faith in our lives to live victoriously. Mountains in your life can be anything that looks big and ugly! Mountains may be that stack of bills, unemployment and no income, your spouse that isn't a believer yet, your child that is in rebellion, no food to eat, no roof over your head, no stability in your life, that bottle of alcohol you can't seem to put down, those drugs that seem to be the only thing to take you away from your problems, that desire to look at things you're not supposed to, or even a move in your life you want to make happen. Or, maybe your ugliness is the filth that floods out of your mouth. Perverted words, cussing, sex talk, words that promote you and exalt you. Maybe it's the way you talk about other people. How you put everyone down because they don't meet "your" standards. There are many mountains of ugliness in our lives, that to us seem impossible to fix, but **God** can fix them! He can fix anything, if you let Him. We have to have faith that God wants to fix our problems, and that He can fix them.

 When we understand His power and begin to walk in it, we will be healthy and we will be able to help others around us. When we realize God is there to help us, not keep things from us, the more we will trust Him in our lives, and the more we will be willing to allow Him to do great things in our lives.

 I encourage you, whatever your mountain may be, the ugliness you see, whatever issue that may be holding you back, give it to God, let your faith carry you through and make you whole! God is good, just taste and see for yourself. I can tell you all day long that a Hershey kiss melts in your mouth, but until you try it for yourself, how can you know for sure? Same with God, I can tell you He will take your mountains of ugliness and issues out of your life because He does it for me, but until you have this experience with God and allow Him to do it for you, you will never fully know! God can take the ugliness in your life, whatever it may be, and make you beautiful and whole again, IF YOU LET HIM!

Let your faith compel you to a place that wants more than what you see. Let it draw you to a place that doesn't want your beauty to just be what you see on the outside. What does the ugliness of our lives removed and Gods beauty instilled in us look like? What exactly does *Gods beauty* bring? It brings humility, modesty, submission, love, and respect for yourself and for others. Ladies, what we have been given is so precious. We tend to take our beauty for granted at times. He gave it to us to share with our husbands. That is if we are married. To those whom decide not to marry, the beauty is for His glory and His glory alone.

Men, your beauty (if you will) is not to draw women in to see how far you can get with them. The words God gives us to speak are not to be taken advantage of and bait a woman's heart so you can sleep with her. Through that ugliness, you are setting her and yourself up for hurt and pain. Stop the ugliness in your life now by giving it to God. Begin to see how God wants us to conduct ourselves for His glory!

When you get dressed to go out, or you're shopping for that new outfit, ask yourself *"Will this outfit glorify you God? Do you see beauty when you look upon me? Am I covered with modesty?"* You see, many women today are in bondage to the lies of the enemy over their self image that they dress to draw attention to themselves. Some may be oblivious to what I am about to say, the fact still remains. Through women's indecency, they become a stumbling block to men and even women. The bible warns us in Matthew 18 about being stumbling blocks. And although you could lie to yourself, and justify it in every way possible to say that you are wearing that outfit because you like it, God knows your *true* intentions behind everything you put on! Psalm 94:11 "The Lord knows the hearts of man." The Lord looks at the heart. Man looks at the outer appearance. Which are you looking for? What approval are you seeking?

You can search forever trying to find beauty among people, even beauty in this world, but *God is the only one who can bring you **true** beauty.* When that beauty comes, it becomes about **other** people. You lose sight of yourself.

It states in Romans 12:3 to not think of yourself more highly than you ought to. I know from experience that when you are wrapped up in yourself, you are ugly in the sight of God. And believe it or not, people pick up on arrogance and pride. They can tell if you're all about yourself, if you think you're the best thing since sliced bread, thinking you're one of the prettiest people on the face of this earth. And surprisingly enough, it's not at all pretty! When you lay down your pride, when you lay down your fleshly high self esteem, you will notice that there is so much more to this life than the way you look. ***Your eyes will become opened to the beauty <u>within</u>.*** Your focus that was once on you, and what God had given you physically on the outside doesn't matter anymore because you know THE EYES of the only one that matters SEES BEAUTY! The One True Beholder! *The Lord will only see beauty to the fullest when your heart is pure.* He will only see beauty when He can look at your mind and see clean thoughts, a purified and clean mind, when He can hear sweet, kind, clean words flowing from your mouth. Words that bring encouragement and build others up not tear them down. Words that come straight from His book He has given you to read and transform your mind with words that will heal the brokenhearted and set the captive free. When He can look upon your heart and see Himself sitting on the throne. He will see beauty when you are walking in and through love! God already knows everything, He made you. When you begin to realize life is about more than just you, about more than just what you

• • •

like, or don't' like, it's about more than what you wear, when you esteem others better than yourself; God will see true beauty when His eyes gaze upon you! You will be able to put someone else above yourself. You will be able to smile when someone else recevies something you may have wanted. You will smile knowing you stepped aside and allowed the light to shine through you onto them! The light doesn't have to be on you. But, through this attitude and beauty, Gods light can't help but be drawn to you also! You will **never** be overlooked when you are walking in the fullness of what God has designed for you to walk in. When you reach this level of beauty with the Lord, what people think about you will no longer matter. Then the only thing you will be concerned about will be if people can see the Lord through you!

Pray this prayer with me. Declare it out of your mouth and see yourself changing from the inside out:

"*Heavenly Father, I come to You in the name of Jesus Christ and I ask that You reveal any ugliness, any impurities in my heart. I want my focus to be on the beauty that lies within my heart and not what I see when I look in a mirror. I realize, God, that it is not about the clothes I put on, the way I fix my hair, or the way I present myself to people that makes me beautiful; but it is my heart that shines forth Your beauty. Remove anything that is not of You, remove anything that does not bring You glory. Lord, I pray that as You look upon me, You will find my heart pure. That You will find clean thoughts, a purified and clean mind. Lord, sit on the throne of my heart, be Lord of my life. Let me walk in this beauty You have made me to be and bring glory to Your name. Let this beauty shine so great from my life that it draws men unto You. Let my life be a life of grace, mercy, love, purity, gentleness, and a compassion for those around me. I thank You for the true beauty that you have given to me. I choose to seek You to find my beauty, and not be consumed any longer of the way the world would view me. You see me God and when You see me, seeking after You, You see me beautiful. That fulfills me Lord. Thank You for loving me, giving Your Son for me so that I may know You intimately. Let me grow in revelation through this book, what You say about me. Let me hide it in my heart and guard it. Open my eyes to see myself the way You see me to be and let me live this life out loving myself, loving the way I look, and loving who You have designed me to be. I will not compare myself to others for You made no piece the same. Everyone is different and I thank You I can enjoy who I am. In Jesus Name. Amen.*"

Chapter 3

Beauty that *speaks*

Out of the ***abundance*** of the heart, the mouth speaks.

"A confident person never has to say a word to be heard."
~ Jeanie Berry

We have established that beauty is not what people see on the *outside*, but its what is in our **hearts**. You see, the bible says in Matthew 12:34 that out of the abundance of the **heart**, the mouth speaks. Let's look at what you are saying. Everything you are saying is coming straight from your heart. Some would say, "I just spoke my mind" but that is not fully true. The thoughts that stay in your mind come from an abundance of what you hide in your heart. Have you ever been around someone who keeps everything in and then explodes with anger because they've had enough? This is what is in their heart. Every time something happens and they just "swallow" it, they swallow it right to their heart. And when their heart gets full, they will spill exactly what they have been feeling and holding onto. So think about it, what are you filling your heart up with? The cares of this world or Gods word that protects you and cleanses you? Are you speaking love, kindness, gentleness? Or are you tearing people apart with the things that are coming out of your mouth?

Instead of "swallowing" your feelings or your thoughts, how about taking them to God and releasing them to Him? Don't allow negative thoughts, feelings or emotions to hideaway inside your heart. You can stay free from them by **quickly** sharing them with God. By doing this you release them from your heart, and He takes it from there! The bible says God will perfect that which concerns you. So no more holding on to things that don't matter or crying over spilt milk or perfume.

We often wonder why women strive so hard to be beautiful in man's eyes. I see times where people treat, honor, and esteem highly <u>pretty</u> people. I can remember in my younger years hardly ever paying for anything. I would have people wanting to go places with me because we would always get everything free. I manipulated many people because of my outer beauty. I later realized, through revelation from the Lord, that it was a spirit (not a good one) working in me and I gave myself over to it. I have always wondered why people treat attractive people different, like they have something so valuable. Pretty people gain ground without even talking to anyone. All for what? They, most of the time, get free things, they get their way, they get treated differently, and when it's all said and done, they manipulate people. No wonder why people are trying to be beautiful! It just seems like the perfect world! I am not saying that all beautiful people manipulate, but I am saying that we all must watch how we claim "favor." But, if all of this is true, and it seems to be in the world we are living in, then how much more do people need to be attracted and drawn to the God in us and strive to be a beautiful image of God's creation?

I want to get you thinking for a minute. The Lord showed me a while back a little about beauty pageants. Now, stay with me and keep an open mind. He asked me, "Why do you think so many girls want to be in pageants and strive to be the prettiest one to the people while she shows off her body and flaunts before them? What is it all for?" And that really struck me hard. At one time I was consumed by pageants, or modeling, and talking about participating in them and even the trophies that I obtained through them. It boosted my self esteem and made me *feel* pretty. And I went back to the question God asked me "For what?" Still reading over and hearing that makes me want to drop to my knees and repent all over again for having that mindset. The answer is obvious -- all for _my_ selfish gain! I wasn't doing it to bring glory to God or to have a platform to share my faith and bring people to the Lord, I was doing it for me.

There is a lot of negativity that comes from pageants whether we realize it or not. Think about it, you have women who go out, try on, and purchase the best dress, fix their hair the best way, walk the runway with the best shake, and their goal is to lure you in to seeing their beauty as they flaunt it. They are out for themselves in the contest, promoting only themselves, and in competition to being the prettiest woman there! Man, that really burdens my heart! And the really sad thing is that we have parents who are raising their little girls up, getting them into pageants the first chance they get. Some have even begun to put makeup on their children at as early as 3 years of age! I even saw a report of 3 year olds hair colored, straightened hair so much it was endangering her hair already, at age 3! The parents are teaching their little girls to be in competition to be the prettiest girl in the group! What do you think that entails for their future? Sounds to me like a bunch of heartache, disappointment, rejection, fear, resentment, hatred, envy, strife, competitiveness, frustrations, anger, and _**unfulfillment**_.

Now, before you put this book down, I am not trying to knock pageants. Please don't get me wrong. I am not here to condemn you for having your child in pageants or wanting to put your child in them. I think if you train your child to understand the fun of it and not the competitive side of it then you could have a good mother and daughter bonding time. I plan on enrolling my daughter in at least one pageant while she is young just so I can see her pretty little smile light up the room. Now will I ever accomplish this, who knows, but I am not totally ignoring the idea. You get what I'm saying? There is a right way and a wrong way to raise your daughter up in this generation today. You can bombard her with the world's views and definition of beauty or you can introduce her early to the one true beholder and the beauty that lies within her through God!

It is our choice as parents to nurture our children in the ways of the Lord and to guide them into all truth. The only way we will be able to show them true beauty is lead them to the one who is the maker of beauty and that is the Lord God Almighty!

Think about this. God asked me this during the outpouring of his revelation of beauty to me. He said "There are many women out there knocking people over trying to get into these beauty pageants because they feel that they have what it takes to compete. If there was such a thing, do you think women today would be able to be in a **Christian beauty pageant**? Do you think you would win 1st place even runner-up?" Talk about your jaw hitting the floor! I still remember when He told me this! It was a Sunday morning and I was getting ready for church. I was in the process of fixing my hair in my bathroom and He began to tell me this. I ran into the kitchen and found the nearest piece of paper and pen I could find because this was so fresh and anointed! It just stirred me up! I mean think about it for a minute! If you are a Christian woman out there, would you consider yourself a candidate for a Christian women's pageant?

Now you realize with this kind of pageant you would be judged according to your *heart*. God would be looking for the pure hearted ones that are not out for themselves, always serving others and seeing to it that other people have what they are in need of. He would be looking to see if you are harboring unforgiveness or offenses towards a brother or sister in Christ, if you are judging them or if you are praying for them. He would be looking for the ones that don't think highly of themselves and that are not selfish; women who walk in love and honor their husbands. A Proverbs 31 woman. He would be looking for the woman who is helping her neighbor win instead of herself! He would be looking at the outfits that are put on and are modest; the clothes and attire that covers what he has created! The role to this pageant would be so different! But man, what a **beauty** pageant that would be! Now that is one that I would like to be in! I would love to participate in one like that where my God can get glory from this pile of dirt He made!

Chapter 4

𝔇arkness revealed

What does beauty mean to *you*?

Take a minute and really search your heart. I even suggest putting the book down a minute and writing down everything that comes to your mind.

"Everything that is hidden in your life will eventually come to the surface and be seen! For there is nothing God does not know, it is not hidden from Him."

~Jeanie Berry

Okay now, look at what you thought or wrote. How much of it was worldly? When I say worldly, I mean it was about appearance, all about the OUTER shell. How much of it was things you have heard beauty was or things you have heard beauty is to look like?

Now, how much of it was INNER? When I say inner, I simply mean *the heart*, God!

In Ecclesiastes, it says that *Beauty Is eternally within the heart.* Whatever God does, it will be eternal. Nothing added, nothing taken away. It's a done deal. God has sealed the deal. Which is to say it has already been.

You see we are so stuck in a trance of what the world defines beauty to be that even when we simply <u>hear</u> the word, we have programmed our minds to immediately think about someone's appearance and outer shell. The bible teaches us that

"man will look on the outer appearance but GOD looks at the HEART!"

Have you ever looked at a person and said, "Man she could be so beautiful but her personality is terrible!" or "Did you see how Lisa was dressed and then walked up like she was just God's best gift to this world. I don't get how someone so pretty can be so ugly!" But that's just it!! People that live their life full of pride, lust, and selfishness bring nothing to the table but straight *ugliness*. <u>And they can't even see it.</u> God is beautiful! Sin is ugly. And the sad thing is, the people that make this category in life, most of them have no idea they are truly ugly. They are so wrapped up and consumed with what GOD has initially given them on the outside that all they can see is what is in front of them, themselves! They are not worried about how they treat someone, or make another person feel. They are living for themselves, and God is not able to get through. The path they are walking on is dark, or very, very dim. There is no light shining from the inside that brightens things in front of them, they are darkened to this! This is truly an assignment of the enemy that slowly makes his way into your thought process. **God is love**.

When we are born again, we give God authority to live inside of us and have His being in us. Through this, just as God is love, we too, will be able to love like God. It is simply seeing through His eyes! This is why you hear things like "I don't know what Sally sees in Bob, I really think he is pretty ugly." or "They really make an odd couple wouldn't you say? I mean, she is so beautiful and totally out of his league, I don't get what she sees in him?" Well my friend, I do! She sees someone who makes her laugh, gives her a shoulder to cry on, lifts her up when the rest of the world is pulling her down, and someone who is totally honest with her and doesn't talk behind her back; a guy who picks flowers off the side of the road because he is thinking about her. We are talking about true beauty! She simply sees the heart of the man, which shines and causes the outer to be breathtaking.

The world has become so blinded to what really counts in these last days. Everyone seems to be fending for themselves in every area of their lives, that the true ugliness is speaking louder than what they realize. There are Christians today, whom you ask if they believe in God and live for Him and they would tell you "Absolutely," yet when they walk away from you they are seeking out the next person they can steal from.

Now, let's take steal and break it down a minute. **Stealing is taking something from someone else.** This means taking a person's money, car, stereo's, TV's, phones, clothes, shoes, jewelry, the list goes on. *Stealing also means,* Christians, taking a person's joy, confidence, peace, happiness, and giving them or feeding them lies, hurt, deceit, frustration, and distrust. Don't get me wrong, everyone is in charge of their own life, but we should be encouraging others, not bringing them down!

When we are not keeping ourselves full of the word of God we have just allowed the enemy to find an "empty place" to dwell in. So when you are talking to that brother or sister in Christ and the whole time you are thinking to yourself "I cannot believe they are talking to me like this" or " Look at what she's wearing, are you serious?", "I can play just as good as her, if not better!" "And she thinks she can sing, I'll show her and everybody else that I'm better!" This is a spirit of pride! And it is dangerous!! I see this trying to operate in churches as well as Christians today.

In the beginning of my walk, I also took a part in this from time to time and believed the lies that would flood in by the enemy. I didn't have confidence in myself, or in God and His word. I didn't know what God said about me and who I really was. I did not have any revelation as what it meant to be a true disciple of Jesus Christ. I did not have the full revelation on the covenant we have with the Father when we accept Him and His will and LOVE for our lives.

This made it easy for the enemy to tear down everything I would get from church services. Hence, I did not read much on my own time. I didn't have a devoted, intimate relationship with God. This meant that I never fully established a strong foundation for God to build on! _I was out for myself, yet still living for God_. And the sad thing was, I really couldn't see it! I was deceived into thinking I was doing right by God by going to church. (Now if you go to Gloryland Church, I know that when you just read that statement underlined above, something rose up inside of you. It is because of the great teaching from the Holy Ghost through our wonderful Pastor.)

You see, you can't do both! You will not ever be able to live for yourself, protect yourself, watch out, look out for just yourself AND LIVE FOR GOD too. The key word in that sentence is _self_. Christians should be praying for others because they know by the covenant and promises of God that they themselves are completely taken care of! They have a trust in God to do what He says He will do for them and their family. They know the authority given to them as a believer, and the victory they have to overcome the enemy in their lives!

The bible says that God shall supply **all** your needs, not some, not only when He's in a good mood, NO! It's every need that is flowing through your head right now! If you are truly seeking the Kingdom of God FIRST, then all these things SHALL be added unto you! When you're looking to further the Kingdom of God, your desires become God's desires. So when you see people's lives being touched and changed forever by the greatness of our God, you will know there is no fulfillment greater than this!

I encourage you to search your heart, ask the Lord to reveal any darkness that may be hidden in your heart.

May the Lord open your eyes to understanding, and may you be delivered from something TO something! People that are delivered from something but not TO something will go back to what they knew prior to. You have the authority to tell Satan to go from your life and he has to obey you. I also encourage you to talk with your Pastor or elders in your church if you would like agreement with this! If you do not have a church, contact someone you know that is walking with the Lord. You may also contact me.

So when you are being delivered from this dark place in your heart, rest upon His word and go TO the right place, In Jesus' name!

Chapter 5

Clothed with His beauty

"Don't settle. You were made to be Royalty."

~ Jeanie Berry

Did you know that you could be walking through life blind-folded and not even know it?

I have walked through life many times blind as a bat and thought I could see clearly! As long as we chose to allow the Lord in our lives and are seeking after His guidance, He *will* show us things that we are blinded to. Some things we just can't see clearly. We have to get to a place where we, as believers, are able to see with Gods eyes! God's eyes see the hearts of people. Those whose hearts are toward Him, He **sees nothing but beauty**!

The Lord said to Samuel,

> "Looks aren't everything. Don't be impressed with his looks and stature. I've already eliminated him. God judges persons differently than humans do. Men and women look at the face; but **God looks into the heart**".
>
> 1 Samuel 16:7(Message)

He sees the best in people because He knows what He has designed us to be. We are fearfully, marvelously, and wonderfully made. We are made in His likeness, made with His hands, made in His image. Wow! What a wonderful thing!

To know that when God looks down upon me; He isn't concerned with what namebrand I am wearing, how my hair is fixed or what color it is. He's not concerned with how skinny I am or the fact I may have a few more pounds than I'm proud of. The only thing He is concerned with is my heart! And in my heart is where the **TRUE BEAUTY LIES**!

• • •

We have no reason to be concerned with our outer appearance when the Lord is the one who clothes us. If we are trying to pick out that outfit that stands out to draw people to our outer beauty we have completely missed it. Don't misunderstand me! I love fashion and nice apperal. But I put it on, in the name of the Lord, knowing my life is a ministry unto Him! Through the way I carry His presence and anointing that is on the inside of me will cause me to shine for Him to be seen in me. There is no clothing in this world that could compare to the clothing God has designed for us to put on!

God says to not worry about what we will put on for He has us and will take care of us, Matthew 6:30.

Let me remind you of the clothing that God has clothed us with.

1. **He has clothed us with gladness**
   Psalm 30:11

He has given us a way to be joyful every day! If we choose to put it on, we *can have* joy and pleasure. God says to Rejoice in Him, everyday. This means wearing a smile! ☺

2. **He has clothed us with strength and dignity**
   Proverbs 31:25

By putting on *strength* He is giving us the power of endurance and resistance to situations in our day.

Dignity gives us moral worth. It's a quality that commands respect. With this covering, we are sure to conquer any tactic of the enemy, and walk out of it with self respect.

• • •

3. He has clothed us with garments of salvation and arrayed us in a robe of righteousness
Isaiah 61:10

Salvation here is the Hebrew word *Yesha'* which means deliverance. So He clothes us with deliverance. And He has drawn us up for battle where we are right standing with Him, a battle where we are on His side! A battle where victory is already ours. With God, we always win! Everytime!

4. He has clothed us with an embroidered dress and put leather sandals on us. He has covered us with *costly* garments, clothed us with silk
Ezekiel 16:10

(I spoke of this earlier, but let's look at it again) This passage was God talking to Jerusalem. He was showing them how when they were born they were not clean. Nobody wanted them, there was no compassion.

They were thrown out into an empty field left abandoned. Yet when the Lord passed by them and saw them struggling in their own blood, He said to them "Live!" *They then grew and matured and became beautiful.*

They were clean but naked, vulnerable, fragile, and exposed. After the Lord passed by again, He saw they were ready for love. After they became His, He cleaned them; gave them a bath and **washed off all the old** blood, and anointed them with oil (made them beautiful). So at this point, they were washed and cleansed from all the old junk/sins.

Now God dressed them in a colorful or embroidered gown and put leather sandals on their feet! In Old Testament, Broidered was work done by a rich and beautiful needle. The badgers skin was simply the best of the best. The eastern people had an art of curiously dressing and coloring the skins of those beasts, of which they made their neatest shoes, for the richest and greatest people. God began to clothe them with the best jewelry. They were provided with everything precious and beautiful: with exquisite clothes. Although if you go and read this passage you will find after God did all of this for them, they turned around and became filthy again!

But this shows us how God takes us from our filth, where everyone else abandons us because of what we have done and throws us out. He takes us in and washes us, cleans us up, and then clothes us with His beauty! He clothes us with HIS ABSOLUTE BEST! We become <u>Royalty</u>! We are His children, a daughter, a son of the King of Kings! It is up to us at this point to **continue** walking in His array of beauty.

5. <u>**He has clothed us with a Garment of Praise**</u>
   Isaiah 61:3

He gives us beauty for ashes, the oil of gladness instead of mourning, and a garment of praise instead of a spirit of heaviness.

So *anything* you are carrying around that seems heavy, God gave us a garment called praise to put on. So you can take off that heaviness by praising God. How do you do that? By thanking God for the things you have, by being grateful and showing gratitude to God. Praise by singing a song to God with thanksgiving. **Shout** Hallelujah! It will make your soul prosper, and the whole time you are putting on Praise! Put some music on, dance before the Lord, get on your face & worship Him. Give Him the praise He is worthy of. Give place to His presence. Back in the older days, people would stand on their rooftops and shout! This was because their rooftops were where people gathered, where they had supper, where there were groups of people, so they would go and SHOUT THEIR PRAISES from their rooftops to be heard. Today, our rooftops would be on the streets, at our work place, at the grocery store, hair salon, any place where we are around people!

6. <u>God clothes us with protection!</u>

The bible says in Matthew 6:30 that God clothes the grass of the field, which is here today and tomorrow thrown into the fire, so will He not clothe us more? We need to do as the Lord says and put on the full armor of God daily.

> "Gird your waist with truth, **put on** the breastplate of righteousness, having shod your feet with the preparation of the gospel of peace; above all, taking the shield of faith with which you will be able to quench <u>all</u> the fiery darts of the wicked one. And take the helmet of salvation and the sword of the Spirit, which is the word of God".
>
> Ephesians 6:13 emphasis added

He wants us to **put on the belt of truth** which holds everything together, **put on the breastplate** which covers your heart, **putting peace on each foot** to carry the gospel gently, and **your shield** which will empower you and keep the enemy from distracting you while you go about all the earth and spread His gospel!

I have been guilty myself tossing outfit after outfit onto my bed because I just did not like how it looked on me. But you know when we get God's perspective and really keep our focus on what He wants us to put on for the day, all of a sudden the clothes you are trying to pick out don't matter much anymore. I mean what better clothes are there than gladness, strength, dignity, ect? So I encourage you, the next time you flip the light on in your closet, and begin to search for that outfit for the day, whatever you put on, put it on in the name of the Lord!

"Getting ready for the day, remember whatever you put on put it on in the name of the Lord!"

~ Jeanie Berry

Chapter 6

Guard your Heart!

"Do not let anything come in that will make you dirty!"
~ Jeanie Berry

Have you ever been in a place where thoughts come into your mind that are not godly?

Thoughts that got you saying to yourself, "If anyone knew this, what would they think?" Have you ever found yourself in a place where you noticed someone was checking you out and you liked it? And your married? The enemy doesn't have new tricks. He uses the same tactics on us every day. His only hope in using it again, is that you would eventually bite the bait he has thrown you. Stay clear from this trap of the enemy. **Guard your heart.** Stay pure in your mind. Allow your thoughts to line up with the word of God and what He says about the situation. I like to throw Philippians 4:8 at the enemy when he tries to come against my thoughts. I choose to think on things that are "pure, lovely, edifying, of a good report, praiseworthy, and true!" The word of God is your weapon. And best of all, there is nothing more powerful!

Your weapon is the word of God. It is SPEAKING it out of your mouth! What good is a loaded gun pulled on your enemy if you don't shoot it? You cannot kill the enemy without shooting! It's the same with the Word of God! You can be filled with the knowledge and words of God, fully loaded and equipped for battle, but if you never speak them out of your mouth to the enemy, then they are null and void of power!

Your weapon will allow you to overcome thoughts and defeat the enemy every time. The only key is, YOU HAVE TO USE IT. Your weapon is the Word of God. Your weapon is speaking and declaring what God says, and not allowing lies to enter into your mind. The bible says to "take every thought captive to the obedience of Christ"

● ● ●

in 2 Corinthians 10:5. God knows that lies and wrong thoughts can come to you. This is why He says to take them captive! Stop them and check them out. Does what you just heard or thought line up with the Word of God? If it does, then receive it. If it does not, reject it and throw it out!

Lies that are allowed in your mind, once they have entered, your mind will begin to process it. Once it is processed, it will then be downloaded into your heart.

That's why the Word of God is so powerful in our lives. That is why God says to "SPEAK" to mountains (situations in our lives). You want to know your most powerful weapon? Your MOUTH. The bible tells us we can have whatever we say, Mark 11:23.

Your words create, just as God created the earth, light, darkness, seas, and even us. In Genesis 1, "GOD SAID." He created everything with His words spoken from His mouth. He didn't just think it, He spoke it. So my question to you is what are you creating with the words from your mouth?

Is there a situation in your life that you want to see God move in? Are you waiting for Him to manifest Himself in a particular situation? Well, my friend, are you giving God something to work with? Because God can only work with His word! The bible tells us in Isaiah 55:11, God looks over His word to perform it, that it will not return back to Him void (uncompleted). If you want to see God move more in your life, my advice to you is change what you are saying or better yet, take His word and speak it out of your mouth! Find out what God says about the situation and declare that. You will see things begin to shift in your life all because you have given God something to work with.

I recall an incident in my life where I became "so busy" that I neglected to read and study the word like I use to. Through this busyness, I found myself drifting slowly away from relationships that were healthy in my life. This brought on some *ugliness*, especially in my marriage.

Because I had not "renewed my mind with the Word of God" my spiritual house was in disrepair. I had begun to get cracks in my wall and I could not see it. The same way the ground will begin to crack when water has not been present, our lives can begin to crack if the washing of the water of the word is not present.

My joy had started slipping. I began to find fault in myself, my husband, my marriage, and everything I was a part of. I was not guarding my heart and the enemy was waiting for a way in. I found myself one day noticing another man. In my mind, I wasn't getting the attention I needed from my husband. He was always too busy anyhow, or when he was home, he didn't want to listen to anything I had to say. All these lies I listened to and received! Then, right in front of me is a man that noticed my presence, smiled at me, watched me, and even flirted a bit. I needed this, right? I mean a woman needs this in her life and if she's not getting it from her husband then…. **NO!!!!!** This is NOT right! It is NOT okay! This way of thinking leads you into bondage, sin, and eventually death.

I had to take my thoughts captive, cast them down, and immediately get God's perspective on the situation. I began to pray and ask God to show me where this came in, so it wouldn't happen again. Now, because I have major revelation in my life, and a strong foundation already built and established through seeking God continually for years, and because I am in covenant with God and my husband; I was able to cut the head off before it developed into major heartache and regret! This very thing has been the beginning of many affairs.

 The enemy uses lies to tell husbands or wives that their spouse don't care about them, that there's no connection, they don't listen, etc. But they are simply that... LIES! It is the BAIT of Satan. I repented and got things right with God, even though some people may think that wasn't anything. To me, I saw the potential of it becoming major. I want to be as close to my number 1 love, God, and my husband as I can be. There is no relationship more fulfilling than the relationship I have with God. He fulfills me in every area of my life! If I ever find myself "lacking" something, or feeling "unfulfilled" I go to GOD, and drink from His everlasting love for me! He completes me! And He wants to complete you too!

Being close with God, eliminates room for anything that is against what He says to stick around. He is light, and in Him there is no darkness! That situation could have done a lot of damage had I not brought it back to the Word of God.

That is why it is so important that we stay in prayer and read the word. We cannot be caught off guard by the enemy. We must stay in fellowship with God. In 1 Peter 5:8, the word of God says "Be alert and of sober mind. Your enemy the devil prowls around *like* a roaring lion looking for someone to devour." Did you see that? He

• • •

goes around **like** a roaring lion; He has no bite and cannot hurt us if we are in fellowship with God. We are God's children and God protects us. Hosea 11:10 reads "They shall walk after the Lord, he shall roar like a lion; for he *will* roar, and the children shall come trembling from the east." The thing is, when God says He will do something, He will do it. God **will** roar for He is the Lion and the Lamb! The enemy can only *try* to do something because he has no power, no sting, unless we listen to him. You hear some people say "I don't need a Pastor or Shepherd in my life to have a relationship with God." This is deception. We all need each other! We all need a Pastor or Shepherd looking after our souls. We are stronger together than when we stand alone. The bible says in Deuteronomy 32:30 that one can set a thousand a flight; two can set ten thousand! The enemy knows we are stronger together! He divides and conquers. His goal is to get you alone so he can do his work on you, devour you, and eventually destroy you. He knows he can wear your faith down when you are by yourself. That's why the Shepherd left the 99 sheep to go after the one that strayed away. The 99 were safe and protected, but that one was being surrounded by wolves preparing for the kill. Luke 15:4 and Matthew 18:12 shows us parables for redemption and how God goes after all that stray from His truth. It shows the protection in numbers. The bottom line is we need each other! You need other people! You need a Pastor to oversee your life and see things that you can not see.

God wants to use all of us; Yes, you too. God has a plan. The only way we can execute His plan is if we follow His instructions and stay in tune with His voice. How do we do this? We do this by staying in fellowship with Him through prayer and reading the word. By going to the church He plants us in and receive the word of God from the man of God He put in our lives. This only develops our character and matures us in the things of the Lord. It prepares us to go out and not only help ourselves, but help others too.

This is where your TRUE BEAUTY is cultivated. Your true inner beauty is cultivated in the presence of the Almighty God. See, what God gives you is not just for you, it is for other people too. Always remember that. So next time God gives you something, don't hesitate to share it!

This all leads back to beauty. We are the most radiant when we have been in the presence of God. We are the most beautiful when we've encountered a moment with Him. Just like Moses. In Exodus 34:29 it says that when Moses came down from Mount Sinai he wasn't aware that his face was radiant because he had spoken to the Lord. His face was glowing and the people knew he had been in the presence of God. Imagine the beauty that was beaming from his face. When you have been in the presence of God, examined your own heart, repented, forgave, and allowed God's mercy and grace to flood over you; *there is no beauty as exquisite as this!* There is no beauty that can speak louder than this. It is a beauty that draws people to you, not for selfish gain, but to glorify your creator, your Father in heaven. God says in John 12:32 "and I, when I am lifted up from the earth, will draw all people to myself." When I read this, I think if I glorify and lift up the name of Jesus, then it will draw people around me to HIM!

God has given everyone this same measure of beauty so that when we step out of our encounter with Him, people will be drawn to us because they will know we have been with the Father. Just as sick people go to the hospital because they know it will have what they need; the same I believe goes for the believers who show they have been with the Lord! They will find people coming to them for answers because they know they will be able to help them!

People will be drawn to God through the beauty He displays through us. In Gods eyes, we are all the same. We are all designed to be a witnessing tool. I think about worship. There have been times I have looked at people having worship and intimate times with God. They may be crying, smiling, you name it, but they have such a beauty and gentleness that is on them.

A person after Gods own heart, seeking God, having encounters with Him, you know, I'm not sure there is **any beauty** that can compare! It's radiant! It's attractive! He wants His children to know that through His eyes we are all beautiful. He wants us to know that each one of us is uniquely made for a purpose. And to Him, THE BEHOLDER'S EYES, we are ALL equally beautiful!

Chapter 7

Glory **IS** the Great Beauty.

Glory
* A distinguished quality
* *GREAT BEAUTY* and splendor
* A ring or spot of light

What is the distinguished quality or characteristic?
IT'S THE LIGHT!

"Be like Moses- let your face glow when people see you, they can't deny you've been with Jesus."

~ Jeanie Berry

As believers of Jesus Christ, we are FILLED with His glory. We are filled with this great beauty! It all comes from within.

In James 2:1 it states:
> "Do not hold the faith (what you believe) of our Lord Jesus Christ, the Lord of Glory, with partiality." (NKJ)

This passage of scripture is talking about favoritism. You have a man decked out in gold, dressed in the richest brand, and smelling good. Then, you have a man caked with dirt, raggedy clothes, smells awful, and poor. They both approach you. You find yourself paying attention to the one dressed nicely and you tell him, "sit here where it's comfortable." To the poor man you say, "Stand there or sit at my feet." Did you not just show favoritism among your brothers? This is what happened in this chapter of James. But you see, God has chosen the poor of this world to be rich in faith and heirs of the Kingdom which He promised to those who love Him!

God says to love your neighbor as yourself. You should see a poor man and have a desire to help him, not shun him away because he doesn't have very much. You should not reject him because he is ugly to you.

James says it clearly, the Lord of Glory. The one who has the power and authority over **great beauty**! Glory IS the great beauty. We're seeking beauty, seeking to be seen in other people's eyes; yet the *only way* to this true beauty comes through the one with the power and authority to give it to us, JESUS CHRIST!

• • •

Those who find themselves always needing attention, acceptance, and compliments are in bondage of a spirit of rejection.

Many times they *are* getting this attention they are starving for but they can't see it! This spirit of rejection causes others to reject you. People with rejection often times have a low self-esteem or low self-image. This comes from listening to complaints or negative remarks from people. "You're fat", "You're ugly", "Your face looks like a pepperoni pizza", "Did your grandma pick out your clothes", "Your hair looks like a rats nest"... you get the picture. When someone has spoken these things they have spoken a "seed" into your mind. **The mind is a POWERFUL place!**

 IF you BELIEVE what they say to be true, you have just taken that seed and planted it into your heart to grow. When that seed grows and blooms you will find yourself thinking and seeing yourself "fat", "ugly", "bad complexion", "dress ugly"... it keeps going on .... *This is why we MUST KNOW who we are in our creator's eyes! When we know this, we will identify with what God says about us and not the trap from the enemy who is trying to rob us of our confidence!*

Just as there are those that think very little of themselves, there are also those that think very highly of themselves. Now being confident in who God has made you to be, is different than being over confident and thinking you are the best thing since sliced bread. People that think this way are simply prideful. They are full of themselves. They have heard and know all too well that they are beautiful, they have the talent, and they have the

• • •

money, the smooth face, on and on ….. But! The bible warns us of what happens if we enter into this state of mind. A FALL IS COMING SOON!

> Proverbs 16:18 " First pride, then the crash- the Bigger the ego, the harder the fall".

In James, we come to realize our beauty comes from God the creator. So, just as He gave it to you, couldn't He just as well take it away? Thankfully, we do not serve a God who gives to us, and then takes it away. It is us, out of our own lusts and desires that we drift away from God and what He has planned for us. You can read James 1:14 to see that for yourself.

 You need to see that there is beauty in everyone, and I can say this confidently because God created them just as He created you! He made us all in His image. We are just so focused on the outer appearance and worldly matters than looking through Gods eyes.

 There **IS** something beautiful about everyone.

Glory in Greek means brightness. I can't help but think about Christmas time and how everywhere you look there is bright Christmas lights shining everywhere! It's the light that draws people in to stop and look and marvel. People go sightseeing because it is simply beautiful, breath-taking and peaceful to look at. Now, take this image and apply it to the church today. We ARE the church! People are drawn by the glory [beauty, light, brightness] IN and THROUGH US. He lives in us.
 His beauty is within us. It lies in our hearts. When we walk out our faith, put His word in our mouth, and have the

great commission on our minds, the *glory* of the Lord shines bright!

 Let us go out and allow the glory, the **true beauty** of the Lord, to shine upon those in darkness.

 Let it be the beauty **within** that they see and can identify with. You see, the outer appearance is only for a moment, but Gods beauty shall never fade!

Chapter 8

Time to get *GOD'S* attention

"Let's get one thing straight PEOPLE DON'T DEFINE YOU."

~ Jeanie Berry

People don't define you. The things that people say about you, does not define who you are. There could be *something* we don't like about ourselves every time we look into a mirror or even try on new clothes in the dressing room. What about the things that we speak out of our mouths? Are we quick to want to change those?

The clothes we wear and the appearance we strive for on a daily basis reflects our heart. The words we speak and the looks we give reflect our heart.

The question you need to ask yourself is **"Do I want people's acceptance or do I want God's acceptance?"**

Being rejected by someone doesn't feel good. There are shallow people that reject you because of what you wear, how you fix your hair, the car you drive, the house you live in, the money you may or may not have, even down to the way you laugh. You can spend your time, money, and effort to changing all of the things people don't like about you or you can come to the realization that God has made you who you are and everything that God has made is good (1 Timothy 4:4 and Genesis 1:31). If you are not 10 lbs underweight, wear $200 outfits, you can still love yourself! If you don't drive a $50,000 car, you can still love yourself! If you don't own a home and all you have done is rent, you can still love yourself!

Realize something right now, GOD DON'T MAKE JUNK! You are important to Him just as you are! You are valuable to Him! You are just the person God is looking for to use and bring His Kingdom to earth.

God looks through our appearance and outer shell straight to our heart. He sees what we are holding onto. Unforgiveness. Bitterness. Jealousy. He sees past our fake smiles down to our frustrations, guilt, shame, depression, lack of self worth, loneliness, and despair. God has given us a temporary body to live in here on earth. It is fun to dress up and enjoy life! I enjoy shopping, trying on clothes & shoes! I enjoy going to the beauty salon and getting my hair done! I enjoy getting manicures, pedicures, and massages! I enjoy dressing up and painting the town. I enjoy putting on athletic shorts, a cut off t-shirt, tennis shoes and throwing my hair up to go play some kind of sport! Those are ways to express who I am. But I am living out of my heart. That is where my true beauty lies. My acceptance is not in how good I am at softball or a sport. My acceptance is not in how pretty I can be in an outfit. My acceptance is not in how many people like me. My acceptance is in my Creator, my Father! I have come to the revelation that GOD LOVES ME just the way I am! He loves everything about me. He accepts me for me. He created me and there is not one thing He does not like about me. I have to get over things that I don't like about myself and realize that He loves it! He loves when I dance for Him! He loves it when I sing to Him! He loves it when I pray and talk to Him! He loves it when I laugh and He loves it when I smile. He just loves me just the way I am! And even better; He loves YOU the same way! He is in LOVE with us!

How are you treating people? Are you all about yourself and your needs or are you really hearing and seeing the needs of your neighbor in front of you? Did you hear that your neighbor was in need? Did you think of a way you could help them? Did you pray for them? Or while they were talking, did all you hear was "me, me, me, me, but then I couldn't….." You see, this is the heart of God. It is about other people. We know that as a child of God, our needs are taken care of. We are blessed to be a blessing to those around us. God sees the content of your heart. Don't let the care of this world choke out the heart of the Father. If there is something that gets into your heart that is not good, then quickly remove it! Get it out of there! It does not belong. It is not who you are. Don't let it stay and trespass. You are a kind, gentle, beautiful being that God created! Stay living out of that!

Enjoy who you are. Enjoy what you like. Be who you were created to be and let your light shine. We are all different. How can you stand out if you are looking, dressing, and acting just like everyone else around you? Your true beauty lies within you. Face it, you are different. You're made to be different. So, enjoy who you are! The people God has placed in your life will love those things about you. They won't try to change you. They will accept you just as you are. So, be true to yourself and be true to God! Live life to the fullest and enjoy it.

"Knowing who you are in God's eyes changes the way *you* see yourself and those around you."   ~ Jeanie Berry

Chapter 9

Worship is Beautiful

You know one thing that really gets Gods attention?
It is our **Worship!**

Worship is our way of expressing ourselves to Him; that being our love, thankfulness, and gratitude. Worship is a way of giving back to God. It's a way of loving on Him. The woman with the issue of blood I spoke of earlier got God's attention! She desired Him! She sought after Him. She pressed through the problems that would be in the way and worshiped Him! That is a true act of worship. She wanted Him, pursued him and didn't let *anything* get in the way!

Hebrews 12:28esv says "therefore let us be grateful for receiving a kingdom that cannot be shaken, and thus let us offer to God **acceptable** *worship*, with reverence and awe,"

John 4:24kjv says "God is a Spirit, and they that worship him must *worship* in spirit and in truth."

Worship is to be in awe of. Worship is an attitude. Worship is finding something you just can't seem to live without and putting it up on a pedestal where you can see it all the time. **Worship is a positioning of the heart.** It's what you think about. It's what drives and moves you. We can Worship God or we can worship an Idol. In our lives, we are worshipping something. It is our choice to make sure we are putting God first. That it is **God**, who is on that pedestal in our lives and in our hearts.

Worship is a huge part of our lives. Although worship is not just about music, it still causes me to think about church services and how we look forward to worship every week.

When the music includes one of our favorite songs we say "The worship was great!" When the music stinks we yawn and wonder why the worship wasn't very good. Some leave churches, even don't become members of a congregation, because of worship styles. Worship is a huge thing!
Have you ever wondered if we're more concerned with what

Worship DOES for us and less concerned with the **object** of our worship and <u>who</u> it's for?

It seems like it's more about what we GET, not what we GIVE. It would be like taking a gift to a birthday party, but keeping it for yourself.

Worship is all about GIVING our lives over to God.

Worship is NOT about the feeling we get when we sing, or the song that gets our feet moving. Worship is not about whether the music is too loud or what's happening on stage. It's not about the instruments, lights or the sound. Worship is all about YOUR heart.

Worship is not about us at all! It's about Him!

We are able to be in His presence at all times because of the blood that Jesus shed for us. His death tore the veil for us to enter into Gods presence and stay there! It's all about what Jesus did for us and that will never change! In His presence, we surrender, love, cry, dream, run, clap, dance, give over, stretch ourselves out to be looked over (Humility), be quiet, listen, kneel, and confess. We look at God and place Him above all else. All because, HE IS worth it!
Life gets crazy and painful, nobody can deny that. Boyfriends, girlfriends, parents, marriage, death, addictions, loneliness; no one is asking you to pretend that those things aren't going on and affecting you. *Don't pretend.* You're just being invited to bring that stuff to Jesus who took care of every bit of it at the cross once and for all! Bring it to God and lay it at His feet. He cares for you! Bring it and gaze upon God who worked with His Son to set **you** free, to heal your broken heart, to heal you of all disease. And as you look at God, allow your response to be – WORSHIP!
I think about some of the songs we sing. One of my

favorites is "You are Good" by Bethel. It says "I *sing* because You are good, I *dance* because You are good, I *shout* because You are good.." Every time I have ever heard that song all I can do is see just how good God has been to me. I am reminded of His faithfulness. I am reminded of His love for me and how He cares so much for me that He lavishes His goodness upon me daily! I love to sing, dance, and shout to that song because I truly worship God for who He is to ME. He IS good to me. His goodness draws me to worship Him. ***It draws me to <u>move</u> when the music begins.*** I can't be still. I can't be quiet. I want to shout and just bust out of my skin if I could because I am THAT in love with Him!

I understand we all have different ways to worship. I am not saying your worship will be like mine. I do know this, a heart that loves on God, singing to Him, and expressing how they feel will not be able to be still and look like their best friend just moved away and they will never see them again! You get me? ***God's presence will cause you to respond!*** <u>Somehow</u>! Sometimes you may not feel like singing, you may not feel like dancing, you may not feel like shouting… but that is when you MAKE yourself! When you put on your praise, you usher in God's presence right where you are! You will begin to feel Him, experience His presence, hear Him speak, or simply enjoy Him in ways you may not have experienced before. Your praise will bust you out of chain or any bondage that has you down! I can promise you that. I have experienced it too many times in my life. I haven't always felt like praising! But, it's those times I am reminded that **God appoints praisers to prepare the atmosphere for His presence to come and scatter the enemy**!! It is then that I am reminded that I am CALLED to worship Him no matter how I *feel*.

When you are in a crowd of people (or by yourself) and you

let your worship out, the atmosphere changes! When many worshippers come together and let their worship out there is an anointing that is released. This anointing seems stronger than normal and God shows up and is able to do things ON the scene! But, it is up to us to release our worship to allow God to move in our services! It's not up to the praise team; it's not up to the pastor or those who are "known" for their worship… it's up to YOU and what you are willing to release!

One of my favorite passages of scripture is found in 2 Chronicles Chapter 20 about Jehoshaphat and how he defeats Moab and Ammon through obedience and praise.

Some came to Jehoshaphat and told him that a huge army was coming against him. What I love is how Jehoshaphat responds. Anytime he received news, he responded with worship! He always went to the Lord to seek direction from Him! He knew that God saw things he could not see. He trusted God and because of his trust, he got instructions and was able to inform his army of what to do next.

God speaks to them saying "Do not be afraid or discouraged because of this vast army. For the battle is not yours, but Gods." It continues with specific instructions from God on what they are to do for **this** battle. After the instructions, in verse 18 it states that Jehoshaphat ***bowed down with his face to the ground***, and then all the people of Judah and Jerusalem fell down in worship before the Lord. Notice, the leader took a worship position and the rest followed. Jehoshaphat's heart was in the right place.

Then the next morning they left out and Jehoshaphat reminded them to have faith in God. ***He appointed men to sing to the Lord and to praise Him*** for the splendor of His holiness as they went out at the head of the army: they sang "Give thanks to the Lord, for His love endures forever."

As they began to sing and praise, the LORD set ambushes against the men of Ammon and Moab and all who were invading Judah, and **THEY WERE DEFEATED**! They ended up destroying one another.

When the men of Judah came to the place where they could overlook the vast army, they saw only dead bodies! Noone had escaped. So, Jehoshaphat and his men went to carry off their plunder, and they found a great amount – more than they could take away! (verses 24-26)

That passage of scripture goes to tell that your praise scatters the enemy and causes what seems to be a VAST army rising up against you, an army that is bigger than what you are prepared for; that GOD will go before you and bring victory- THROUGH YOUR PRAISE!

Another awesome passage I love that displays a true heart of worship is the woman with the alabaster jar!

Luke 7:36 – 50 tells it so well. She was a sinner. She was shunned by the Pharisees and was not to even approach Jesus because of the judgment they had upon her. She had been saving up some very costly oil and heard that Jesus was sitting at the table with the Pharisees.

"She stood at Jesus' feet behind Him weeping; and she began to wash His feet with her tears, and wiped them with the hair of her head; and she kissed His feet and anointed them with the fragrant oil." Luke 7:38
The Pharisees spoke to Jesus trying to explain who this

woman was and how He shouldn't be letting her touch Him! But Jesus' response is so precious! **He received her.** *Sin and all.* Jesus begins to teach Simon something about forgiveness and the gratitude of it. And then he says:

"Do you see this woman? I entered your house; you gave Me no water for My feet, but she has washed My feet with her tears and wiped them with the hair of her head. You gave Me no kiss, but this woman has not ceased to kiss My feet since the time I came in. You did not anoint My head with oil, but this woman has anointed My feet with fragrant oil. Therefore I say to you, her sins, which are many, are forgiven, for she loved much."
(verses 44 – 46)

She saw **Jesus** as the one she needed! She knew He would not push her away or reject her and I believe she stood there at His feet, in His presence, weeping because she felt the love He had for her despite what she has done. He took her out of her filth, forgave her, and gave her a new start! It was her faith that made her whole! She truly expressed an act of worship!

I love to dance to the song "Alabaster Box" by CECE WINANS. This song puts me in the image of this scene and me standing there with MY alabaster box. All of my sins that he has forgiven and cleansed me of, and the frame of mind I was in when He picked me up and hugged me are sitting in my alabaster box laid at His feet! When people rejected me and pushed me away because of the things I had done, Jesus received me!

 It says "You weren't there the night He found me, you did not feel what I felt when He wrapped His loving arms around me, and you don't know the cost of the oil in my alabaster box." So powerful! *We can't begin to think we know where somebody else came from. **Everyone has a past.*** I am so thankful that God has said to me "Your sins are forgiven. Your faith has made you whole. Go and sin no more!"

Look at the woman with the issue of blood. She pressed her way through a crowd of people that didn't accept her. But she didn't care! Her worship was so great and she _knew_ she needed an encounter with Jesus! She didn't let **anything** stand in the way. Because of that, she received what she needed!

Look at Zacchaeus in Luke Chapter 19. He didn't let his problem of being little keep him from seeing Jesus! He found a way to make what he needed to happen, happen!

People didn't like him because he was the chief tax collector; therefore there was not any that would help him. He was on his own if he wanted to see Jesus! He found a sycamore tree and climbed up to see Him. Zacchaeus **positioned himself** to see Jesus! Jesus spotted him up there and told him to make haste and come down because He was going to stay with him. There were many people there but Jesus pointed out Zacchaeus. I believe it was the act of worship Zacchaeus responded with when he was in Jesus' presence. It says that the crowd was complaining because Zacchaeus was a sinner and Jesus was leaving all of them to go be with "him".
Zacchaeus had worship time with Jesus. Zacchaeus spoke and told Jesus his heart and what he was doing. Through his repentance, salvation came to his house that day.
Look at Mary and Martha in Luke Chapter 10:38-42. Mary

and Martha sat at Jesus' feet and heard His words to them but Martha was so **distracted** by other things that she couldn't press in and receive in His presence. Mary stopped and made time for His presence. She displayed an act of true worship. When Martha went to Jesus to tell Him what Mary was doing was wrong, He corrected her and told Martha she needed to stop worrying about so many things and enjoy His presence too!

I could continue to show you example after example in the bible of all different acts of worship! Worship is about your heart. It's about your attitude toward God and His Son Jesus. I will leave you with one more example that speaks volumes to me, the widow woman.

Jesus was looking as all the rich dropped in their offerings but there was **_a certain woman_** that caught Gods attention! The widow woman brought up 2 mites and placed it in the offering. Two mites today would equal about 2 pennies. That was all she had. She gave all she had! Giving all you have does not mean you go and dump out your bank account to show God you mean business and worship Him! Giving all you have means "Here God! You can have it all! Take it all, all I want is YOU!" God does not _need_ our money, He does not _want_ our money; God wants our hearts!

Jesus said that day:
"Truly I say to you that this poor widow has put in more than all; for all these out of their **abundance** have put in offerings for God, but she out of her poverty put in all the livelihood that she had." Luke 21: 1-4

Your offering SPEAKS!

When you give out of your abundance, you have to be cautious that you are not just giving something that doesn't mean anything to you. Our offering should speak to us and to God. Money is not how we measure our worship. It's not the amount we give. **It is the cheerful and gratitude <u>heart</u> we are bringing it with.**

Giving to God is another act of worship. God has set up a principle for us to honor Him and keep Him first in our lives. That principle is called the tithe. Malachi 3 is a good teaching on the tithe and how God sees it.

God says "Will a man rob God? … He has robbed him in **tithe** and **offerings**… bring **all** the **tithes** into the **storehouse**, that there may be food in My house."(emphasis added)

Stop right there. WE are His house where He dwells. We are the temple of the Holy Spirit where God lives. Food is the living word of God. It is what keeps us alive Spiritually.

So, when we bring Him the tithe, we are allowing His living word to live and **develop** us on the inside. We must let the tithe go. It leaves our hands into the one who God has sent to watch over and help us grow in Him and the revelation revealed to us in His word.

God goes on to say "Try me in this! See if I will not open for you the windows of heaven and pour out for you such blessing that there will not be room enough to receive it!" (emphasis added) Then He says that He WILL <u>rebuke</u> the devour (satan) for our sake that he cannot come in and destroy the fruit of our ground! That means satan will not be able to come in and steal or take **_anything_** from your life when you honor God with your first fruits.

Tithe is 10% of the money you receive. You simply, get your money, take out 10% and give it back to God. By doing this, you are saying "God I know YOU are my source. I live for You, I honor You, I worship You... I am acknowledging that YOU are the one who has made this possible. You are where all blessings flow from. I am coming back TO YOU and giving You what belongs to You." It's not just the tithe – it's our heart!

Our heart belongs to God. Our heart can get wrapped up in serving ourselves, serving this world, or serving God! So, by bringing God what belongs to Him, we are bringing Him our hearts! Offering is anything above the 10% that belongs to God. Offering can be money but offering can also be things you own that you give to someone else.

Anything you give, tithe and offering, is your seed! When you plant your seed, water it, it will grow and produce a harvest in your life and you will reap blessings! **This is an act of worship!** It is all about your heart. Giving to God is not so you can get something back. When you give your tithe, you don't give it so that God will bless you. God blesses His children, period. When we give to God, His response is to give back! It is an act of honoring God. You have to truly see that when you give your tithe and offering, you are giving it in the name of the Lord and God will look over it to make sure it produces in your life. His word says that you will either serve God or mammon. Mammon is money. By acknowledging God with your finances, you are making mammon (or money) bow it's knee to God. You are telling the enemy that GOD is who you serve, not this world and the things in it. You are

• • •

81

letting satan know that God is your source and you know that all blessings flow from Him. You are showing that you TRUST God to be your provider, not your job or people. You respond with a true act of worship!

Your praise/worship is more significant to **overcoming** than you realize! That is why the enemy comes against it so hard. He knows if he can keep you still, keep you quiet, keep you holding onto your money, and stay in your little box... he will have a way to keep you from going anywhere! All it takes is a shout, a dance, a lifting of your hands, a swaying to the beat or even a full out run or dance! All it takes is allowing your finances to flow from your hands to someone else. It breaks the hold of the enemy and allows God to FLOOD in and take over! You become less and God becomes more. Don't believe me? Try it! ☺

Worship gets Gods attention! Your Praise, Worship, Tithe, and Giving is so powerful and important to your spiritual walk! Don't allow the enemy to shut you up! Overcome by stepping out, trusting God, and acting on His word!

WORSHIP! WORSHIP! WORSHIP! WORSHIP!

"Worship the King of Kings, the Lord of Lords! He is so worthy of your praise! Sing songs to Him. Dance before Him. Love on Him. Lift your hands and welcome Him!"
~ Jeanie Berry

Pray this prayer with me:

"Father God,

I thank You for Your Son. I thank You for Your love and for Your mercy, grace, and forgiveness that You bestow on me. This book has opened my eyes to see beyond the outer appearance of man and to look at the heart as You do. To see the best in people and love them as You love them, and to see the best in me as You see me to be. Help me to not get put out with people because they are not like me. Help me to value them and the gifts You have given to them just as the gifts You have given to me. I thank You that I can see clearly where my true beauty comes from. I repent for trying so hard to fit in to what the world's standards of what beauty is. I know now, that You have created me, made me in Your image, and I am beautiful! I know now that it is not what I put on but it is what is hidden in my heart. I will hide Your word in my heart and seek Your presence daily. I pray that You remind me each day to guard my heart diligently for out of it flows the issues of life. I pray that I am Your glory released here on earth. That when others look at me, or are even in my presence, that they will experience Your glory, Your beauty, Your love. I pray that when people look at me, they see You. I pray that I may take this information from this book and share it with other people so they too can see their true inner beauty as I do now.

I thank You for Your word. I love You and I choose to live this day forward honoring You in everything I do.

I pray this in Jesus name. Amen"

God Speaks about *Inner* Beauty.

Here are scriptures to read and feed your spirit man. Confess out loud the truth about Beauty.

*These scriptures will come straight from the bible and some will have extra confessions prompted by the Holy Spirit.

I will not let my adorning be external – the braiding of my hair and the putting on of gold jewelry, or the clothing that I wear – but I will let my adorning be the hidden person of the heart with the imperishable beauty of a gentle and quiet spirit, which in God's sight is very precious.
1 Peter 3:3-4 esv

I adorn myself in respectable apparel, with modesty and self-control, not with braided hair and gold or pears or costly attire, but with what is proper for women who profess godliness – with good works. I understand Lord, it is not wrong for me to wear costly clothes, or jewelry, or even braid my hair. It is wrong for me to desire those things above You. I choose to be modest and live in such a way that is pleasing to You. I choose to desire You above anything I put on and desire to wear. It is not about my appearance and how I appear to others, it is how I look and appear to You.
1 Timothy 2:9-10esv and added

I am altogether beautiful; I am Gods love; there is no flaw in me. For I was made in Gods image, in His perfect likeness. God does not make mistakes. I am fearfully and wonderfully made.
Song of Solomon 4:7, Genesis 1:27, Psalm 139:14

Charm is deceitful, and beauty is vain, but a woman who fears the Lord is to be praised. I am a one who fears the Lord.
Proverbs 31:30esv and added

I praise you, for I am fearfully and wonderfully made. Wonderful are Your works; my soul knows it very well.
Psalm 139:14esv

Just as God said to Samuel, I remind myself not to worry about my outer appearance as much as my heart. Because it is people who look at my outer appearance but it is God who looks at my heart.
1 Samuel 16:7esv and added

I am patient, I am kind; I do not envy or boast; I am not arrogant or rude. I do not insist my own way; I am not irritable or resentful; I do not rejoice at wrongdoings, but I rejoice with the truth. It is love that bears all things, believes all things, hopes all things, endures all things. Love never ends and my love will never end.
1 Corinthians 13:4-8esv and added

Because I look to God I am radiant, and my face shall never be ashamed.
Psalm 34:5esv and added

I am (or will be) an excellent wife. I am far more precious than jewels. The heart of my husband trusts in me, and he will have no lack of gain. I do him good, and not harm, all the days of my life.
Proverbs 31:10-31 and added

I am not anxious about the clothes I put on. I consider the lilies of the field, and how they grow and how God supplies all they need. I know He loves me more than they, and He will provide for me too.
Matthew 6:28esv and added

Blessed are the pure in heart, for they shall see God. Therefore, I shall see Him.
Matthew 5:8esv and added

I live by the Spirit, therefore I walk by the Spirit.
Galatians 5:25esv

I have the fruit of the Spirit. I produce love, joy, peace, patience, kindness, goodness, faithfulness, gentleness, and self control. I produce after Gods kind.
Galatians 5:22(different translations and added)

For to set my mind on the flesh is death, but to set my mind on the Spirit is life and peace. Therefore, I do not set my mind on the flesh

but I choose to set my mind on the things of the Spirit. Because of that, I have life and peace.
Romans 8:6esv and added

Strength and dignity are my clothing, and I laugh at the time to come.
Proverbs 31:25esv

I put on the whole armor of God, that I may be able to stand against the schemes of the devil.
Ephesians 6:11esv

You formed my inward parts; You knitted me together I my mother's womb. Therefore, God You have known me since the beginning. You created me with a plan and a purpose. You have plans to give me hope and a great future. I am not a mistake. You know the numbers of hair I have on my head and You love me.
Psalm 139:13esv, Jeremiah 29:11, Luke 12:7niv and added

For God so loved the world, that he gave His only Son, that whoever believes in him should not perish but have eternal life. I believe in your son, Jesus.
John 3:16esv and added

If I confess my sins, You are faithful and just to forgive me my sins and to cleanse me from all unrighteousness. I repent Lord. I repent for ------------ and I thank You that You forgive me and wash it away as if I had never done it. You give me a new chance, a new life. You put your Spirit inside me and live in me. I will choose to walk by your Spirit and I will not fulfill the lusts of my flesh. I will honor and please You all the days of my life. I choose to serve You, my household will serve You all the days of my life and our life. I choose life. I lay down my pride and humble myself before Your mighty hand and You lift me up. I love You God and I thank You for this new beginning. In Jesus name, Amen.
1 John 1:9esv, 2 Corinthians 5:17, Galatians 5:17, Joshua 24:15, 1 Peter 5:6, and added

Don't be ashamed to be YOU. Don't be afraid to be YOU. Don't hold back; but enjoy being YOU!

You are beautiful just the way you are! Embrace it. You are unique. There is not another like you. Be like God and shine!

Don't be afraid to be different. You are fearfully and wonderfully made. You have a unique purpose and calling that God has planned specifically for your life; that only YOU can fulfill. Join with other believers and add your piece to the ultimate puzzle – the finished picture is breath taking!

Life is too short to focus on all the things you don't like. Think on those things you do like and give God what you don't. ENJOY LIFE! Don't let life pass you by. Don't let the people God has given you pass you by either. I am so thankful for my husband who has been by my side through my journey pursuing God. He has not given up on me. He has looked past the things I do not like and he sees me the way God sees me. I am so very thankful for such a blessing! If you have someone in your life, know God has sent them to you. Love them as Christ has loved you and given Himself for you. Pursue love and don't give up!

A LOVE WE WILL FOREVER SHARE!

Thank you Jesus!

Now, enter into the rest God has for you! Know who you are. Be who you were made to be. Shine so bright for God for all the world to see. Believe that God loves you. Don't give up. Fight the good fight of faith. Cling tight to the words of our Lord. Hide them in your heart and speak them out of your mouth. And live your life as unto the Lord. Peace be with you.

AMEN!

Made in the USA
Columbia, SC
02 January 2020